World War II: Secret Agent

Written by Jillian Powell

Contents

Wanted: secret agents

It's 1941, two years into World War II. Germany has **invaded** most of Europe. Britain needs secret agents for **special operations** in enemy countries.

Your job will be to destroy enemy targets and work with
resistance fighters against the enemy.

Can you pass the training and become a secret agent?

Physical training

You'll begin with hard physical training.

You need to be strong and fit as you'll be parachuting into enemy countries and you may have to fight enemy forces.

You'll be sent to secret training grounds in Scotland where you'll train by climbing mountains and **abseiling** down them.

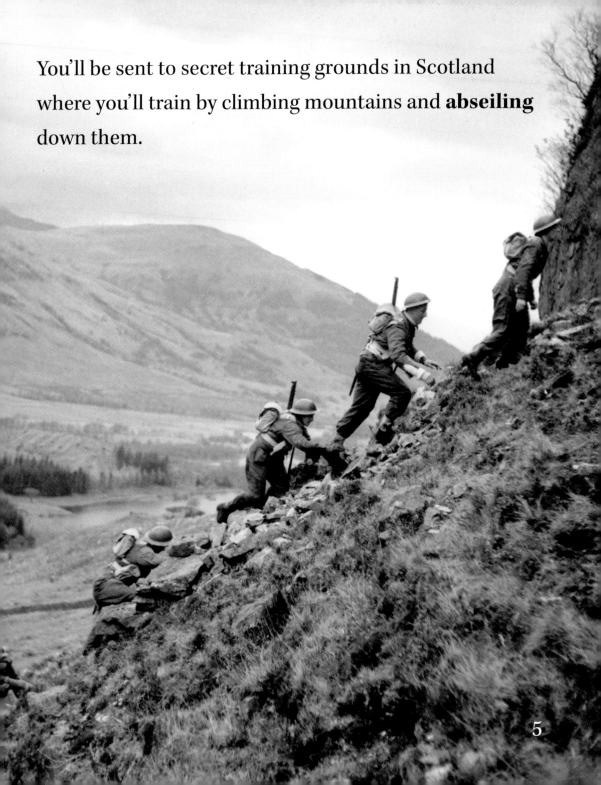

Combat skills

Next you'll practise **combat** skills. You must be able to defend yourself without weapons against an enemy.

Your work will be dangerous and you
must learn to use secret weapons, too.

dagger – strap it to your arm or leg

pencil with blade inside

pen containing **tear gas**

Explosives

You'll learn how to destroy enemy targets such as bridges and railway lines. This will make it harder for the enemy to move troops or supplies around.

You'll **smuggle** hidden explosives into enemy countries and use them to blow up important buildings and transport links.

a bridge in France that has been blown up to stop the enemy using it

Parachute training

Next, you'll begin parachute training. You'll learn to parachute jump and land safely.

You'll carry a spade tied to your leg so when you land you can bury your parachute and jump suit. No one must know that you've landed in enemy countries.

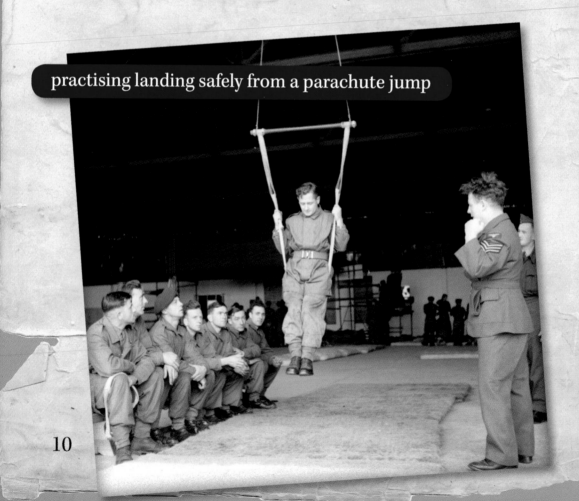

practising landing safely from a parachute jump

learning how to
parachute jump

11

Secret messages

You must learn to send secret radio messages and signals from countries **occupied** by the enemy.

radio-telephone for sending secret messages

You'll need to exchange information with other secret agents and local resistance fighters without the enemy finding out. You'll use codes to send map readings, report on operations or instruct resistance fighters.

This radio set is hidden in a biscuit tin.

A secret letterbox is hidden in this gate post.

Map-reading

You must learn to map-read and use a **compass** as you'll need to find your way, alone, around countries occupied by enemy forces.

You must keep your maps and compass hidden from the enemy as you may be captured as a spy.

This map can be hidden inside this hairbrush.

Secret life

You must learn to live a secret life in enemy countries. You must dress, act and speak like a local citizen or an enemy soldier, so you are not found out as a spy.

Wear these decoy feet to disguise your boot prints when you land on beaches. The enemy will think they are footprints of local people.

You may be sent to countries that Germany occupies in Europe or to the Far East where Japan is fighting against **the Allies**.

17

Behind enemy lines

If you pass your training ...

A pilot working on special operations will fly you to your drop-off point behind enemy lines.

An aeroplane like this one will take you to the starting point of your mission.

Now you are on your own. Are you ready to be a secret
agent and help win the war for your country?

Glossary

abseiling	using a rope to get down from a high place
combat	fighting
compass	an instrument that shows which way is north, south, east and west
invaded	sent soldiers into a country and took it over
occupied	taken over by another country
resistance	standing up to an enemy by secretly ruining their plans
smuggle	sneak things into a place secretly
special operations	secret spy missions run by a British organisation called the Special Operations Executive
tear gas	gas that makes people's eyes run so much that they can't see
the Allies	the countries that supported Britain in World War II

Index

Becoming a secret agent

You must be strong and fit.

You must be able to defend yourself.

You must know how to use secret weapons and explosives.